Chaos of Love

Penny Lamon

Chaos of Love © 2023 Penny Lamon

All rights reserved.

No part of this publication may be reproduced, stored in a retrieval system, or transmitted, in any form or by any means, electronic, mechanical, photocopying, recording or otherwise, without the prior written permission of the presenters.

Penny Lamon asserts the moral right to be identified as the author of this work.

Presentation by *BookLeaf Publishing*

Web: www.bookleafpub.com

E-mail: info@bookleafpub.com

ISBN: 9789357748124

First edition 2023

DEDICATION

For Azrael...

My heart.. My Soul...

My Single Bullet...

PREFACE

There's this theory out there I read about in a book by Michael Connelly, where FBI agent Rachel Walling falls in love with crime reporter Jack McEvoy, it's called the single bullet theory of love. It's the theory that one person can pierce your heart so deeply, like a bullet to the heart, that no matter what happens after you meet them, nobody will ever come close to equaling the love you have for that one single human bullet. It might be the greatest love failure of your life in the end, but you will continue to love them more deeply than anyone else for the rest of your life. If you're lucky you'll never discover what it means or feels like to live without them. I've not been that lucky, yet the love is still there. It's been years since I was even in his presence, but I can still feel him, hear his voice. The sound of home that voice. And though he comes and goes from my life at times, I'll always have the hope that one day he'll just stay and never leave. However unlikely that is, it's true. No one will ever compare to the love I have for him. My past is full of nightmares and horrors, sprinkled with the memories of the love I have for him. It may not be a fair standard of comparison for those who have been in my life since him or for my future but we all have our flaws don't we.

Absolute Must

I love...
the depth of color in the silence of the abyss...
the passion in anger, of the argument ended with a
kiss...
the grief that's hiding in the shadows of a wounded
soul...
the pain that's hollowed out it's niche in gold...
that first moment of love that sinks in like a poison
dart...
the jagged cracks stitched together, holding a broken
heart...
that spectacular look that can dry flooding tears on
cheeks...
the decay of sorrow in winter as spring finally
defeats...
the darkness that radiates out when an epic love is
lost...
or the fire that burns in the intellect, learning at any
cost...
all the senses that awaken in deeply held desires and
lust...
and that all those things don't exist without love, for
love, love is an absolute must...

Serendipity

She's s a chance encounter, luck of fate you will
decide... It's not luck for her but a broken path by
which she did arrive...

A slave to empathy, the emotion hiding in another's
soul... She'll dig deep within the grave they're buried,
to bring them from the hole...

Like a junkie with a fix, she can smell desire when its
near... She can taste the passion emanating from your
fear...

She hears through the anger to the greatness you can
be... If you choose to let her dig, she'll show you what
she sees...

The color of your soul is a beacon that guides her
through the dark... She'll put your broken pieces back
together, smooth over the mark...

Healing the pain of others, heals a little of her own...
Yet they walk away with all that she has shown...

Teach them to love, heal the wounds they hold
within... She'll bleed picking up the pieces cut away
in the end...

Leaving her empty and alone, inside the chaos she can't escape... She's collared to the search for a home, the one who holds her fate...

The one who will diminish her wounds, not an option set aside... The one who stays to hold her heart, protected and sanctified…

Singularity

what i know is a scratch on the surface, that brings a
desire i don't want to fight...
leaving vivid images in my mind in the darkest hours
of night...
i've watched you for awhile, the perfect flaw in a
gradually growing scene...
an intriguing singularity within the crowd, that's
become my favorite dream...
with a mind that has no boundaries, you have
matched the words i thought i had sedated...
awakened a passion that i intentionally kept crated...
you gave me a moment and i felt the hesitation you
fought to hide...
cautious of the consequences, careless enough to feed
your pride...
a thousand images, just a little time, flash ceaselessly
in my mind...
bringing the feeling of your skin back to life...
i'd like to scratch a little further, dig deep into your
soul...
feel you move on the inside, match the passion
breaking through the fold...
my view may be distorted but you've never seemed to
mind...
that pedestal i've put you on has no expectations to
uphold or find…

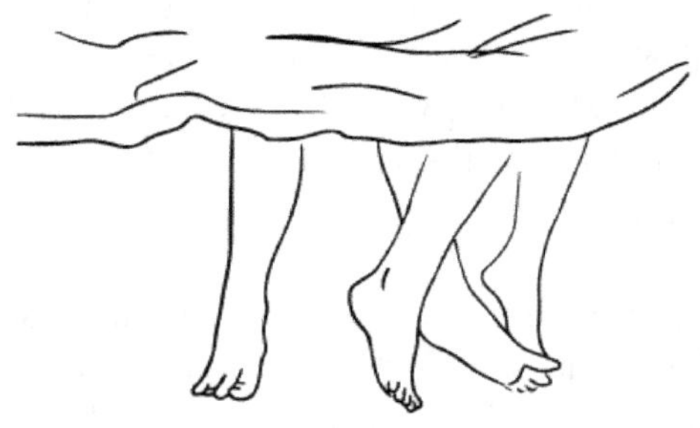

Work of Art

tell me who you are, that i don't wish to look away...
i've seen your kind before, you intrigue me in every
way.. shadowed by the coming night, you glisten in
the dark.. silhouetted in the trees, you stare back like
a work of art..

there's a soul in your kind that resonates out across
any night.. creating unfiltered images that block out
everything else in sight.. with a passion and intellect
that can illuminate the dark.. you're perfectly flawed,
like a work of art..

caught up in the moment, you smile and nod your
head.. a picture worth a thousand words, you've never
even said.. and still you stand there, statued,
captivating from the start.. it's open to interpretation,
like a work of art..

a need to touch the canvas, demands that i remain.. a
lifetime of instant visions that can sustain this this
abstracted domain.. sparking intricate lines of desire
that painfully make their mark.. the branding at the
end, a signature on a work of art..

watching as you walk away, a fire kindles deep
within.. i'd like to know more about you, the history
of your skin... to trace the edges of your soul and
heart.. to feel the scars that made you a work of art..

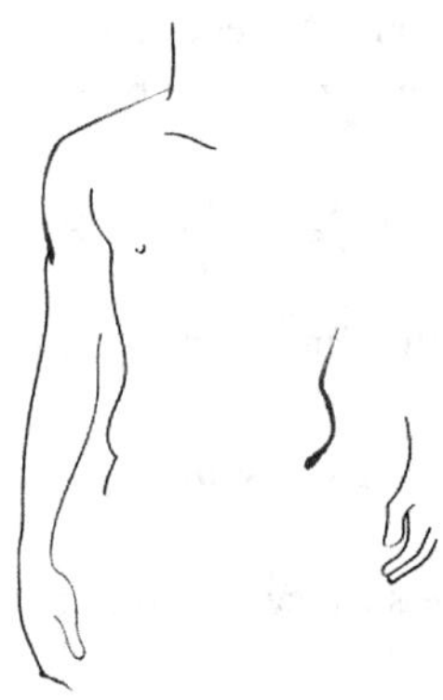

Azrael

it was years ago the desire did begin.
for the drug i dream about digging my fingers in.

for that touch that always set my skin on fire.

to smell that poison that penetrates my skin.
to taste the iron and salt of the blood rushing within.

for that look that brought a burning desire.

it's an aftertaste that lingers making the days bitter
and sweet.
a hunger that starves my soul making it weak.

that scratches the surface naked and lain.

a residue painted on my lips in perfection of endless
heat.
the ecstasy of my dreams and a long treasured treat.

that bites in an equal amount of pleasure and pain.

Heart's Domain

Silence becomes a constant as the days drift by,
I remain in solitude with no tears to cry.
Your presence restores safety to what was taken from
my mind,
Your voice caresses the edges of my soul which no one
else could find.
You held me and the world seemed to disappear,
I lost myself and for a moment there were no tears.
Everything seemed safe, illusions no longer real inside,
The fear that once existed had finally died.
Your gentle touch, the softness of your soul,
Took away the pain and the feelings of cold.
For the moment the fears subsided and pain was denied,
Knowing that at any time from you I could not hide.
You take the pain and from me you hold it away,
And in the confines of your heart is where I wish to stay.
So if you will, allow me to remain,
In the shelter of peace within your heart's domain.

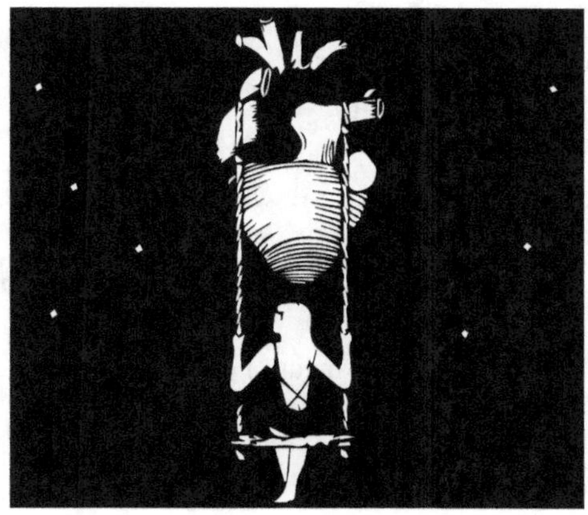

Unchained

you're everything to me in a world that's always been
so wrong...
that darkness wrapped around the ashes of my soul,
gave me a home...
allowed me to shine beyond the nightmares that have
scarred my heart..
gave me peace in the chaos of a world i've never
belonged...

and then you were gone...

the darkness you fight with day and night, i crave to
cover all that is torn...
it protected the good within me, let me feel safe and
warm...
i've felt every emotion you can never bring yourself
to display...
i see the color of your soul piercing through the
darkness above...

and then you were gone...

you took my heart and soul when you slipped silently
away...
unchained me to the chaos i can't seem to tame on my
own...
i'd give everything if it meant i could forever touch
your face...

protected and home, against the nightmares i wake
from everyday...

just to feel home...

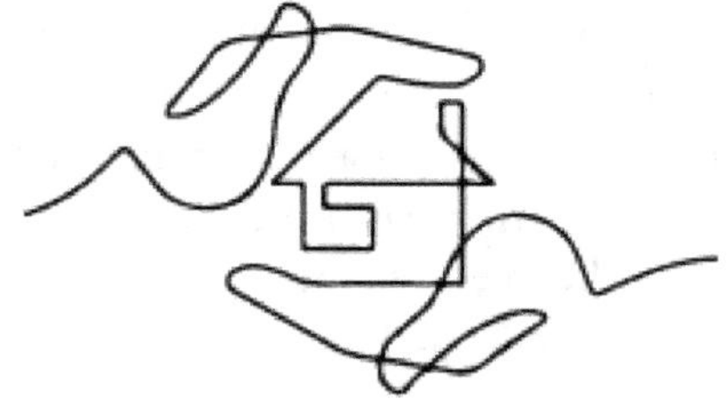

Save Me

save me from myself if there's something left of me
to save.. capture me from the chaos of that which i
cannot stave.. give me the sanctuary that i may
forever dwell.. cradled from the pain and torments of
a soul i cannot seem to quell..

breathe for me when i suffocate from the screams that
choke me in the night.. don't let me drown in this
nightmare that doesn't end with mornings light.. show
me the sanctuary where silence can block deaths
knell.. and shelter me from the pain and torments of a
soul i cannot seem to quell..

would you abandon me to the thoughts that hold me
as a slave.. withhold the addiction of you that every
hour i crave.. will you lock away the sanctuary that
can keep me from dying in this hell.. leave me
bleeding within the pain and torments of a soul i
cannot seem to quell..

Essence of my Soul

time goes on forever as i occupy this empty space..
days pass with a sallow recognition of this place..
your face still echoes in the memories i retain..
wishing within my arms you still remained..

captured by another, not a thought that came to me..
too late to change the chaos now that has come to be..
little reminders that turn in to sleepless nights.. bring
breathless hours and endless sights..

caught up in transition, stuck by simple mistakes..
wanting back what i helped create.. missing the joy
that came with your very presence.. you're a part of
my soul, the survival of my essence..

bonded and separated, can love transcend distance..
strangled breaths make up a painful existence..
nightmares torture that you will never return.. time
doesn't travel backwards, i don't want to relearn..

how do i live without you, will divinity protect.. will
the absence of you bring me again to neglect.. safe
and whole, will i see you again.. striving for
something greater, chaos at an end..

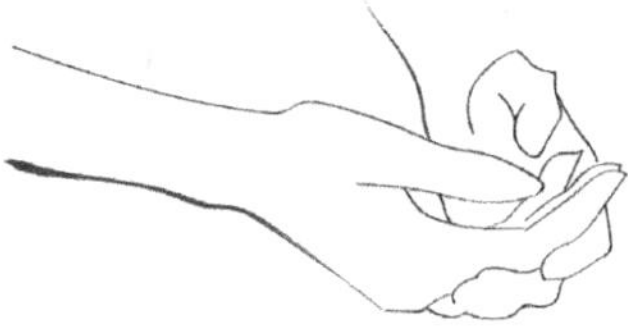

In Dreams

you live and breathe away from me, yet alive inside my endless dreams.. i long to live there, within the actions of fiends.. touching the lust and knowledge i can't obtain awake.. love that exists after dark where nothing is at stake.. if you felt me move from within, would all be ripped apart? would the dream i wake from become the longing you suppress in your heart? lifetimes will have been lived before we'll ever reunite.. crossroads explored in search of the magic we created at night.. when all that existed was a love and passion that burned and paralyzed our souls.. an ecstasy that stills binds me and offers sanctuary from the cold.. i always find you in a flicker of darkness holding what i wish to achieve.. in a dream where you consume me in countless ways and i long to never leave.. there's no boundary between our souls in the darkness of sleep.. entwined with you there's no restrictions on the actions we reap.. where we allow no interference in the essence we create.. actions without discretion, where nothing else can gravitate.. as all the senses come alive again and we're lost to those without.. to touch in dreams what only reality holds in doubt.. to lick off the lust on your lips, bite the artery of pleasure and pain.. to feel you from within and taste what only in dreams i can attain..

Whiskey Residue

i can still feel it, the connection hasn't been lost..
when i dream of you, pictures in a shadow box..

each frame a different scene from the years of past..
ghosts that haunt the present, linger and grasp..

the memories are jagged, torn from years of twisted
pain.. blocked out by my soul, hiding the bloody
stains..

taking pieces of you from me, that nightmares have
replaced.. a single touch from you that left my heart
encased..

a residue left behind that i've never been able to wash
away.. no amount of whiskey can fill the hole that
refuses to decay...

i hear your voice in every silent breath i take.. i see
your shadow in the dark as i lie awake..

you're in my dreams and hiding in every thought.. i
keep moving on but i think my soul's been bought..

The Hollow

there's always been a power in you that resides deep inside.. drawing me within the darkness you try so hard to hide.. it was there i found a hollow that held me while i slept.. enveloped in the blackness of you, it always did protect.. you shielded me in fire and burned the pain away... cradled me with whispers that shook your own domain.. you touched the edges of my slaughtered soul with an easy light.. and it conflicted with your darkness to have me in your sight.. it was in that hollow i found you, bloodied broken and bare.. where i saw the love and passion you had buried there.. under years of anger and in silence to the pain.. i tried to stitch together the pieces that remained.. to help uncover the light the darkness had swallowed whole.. to help you see the path that led me straight into your soul.. to show you there's a balance to what you carry as a plight.. that i'll always need that blackness to protect my inner light..

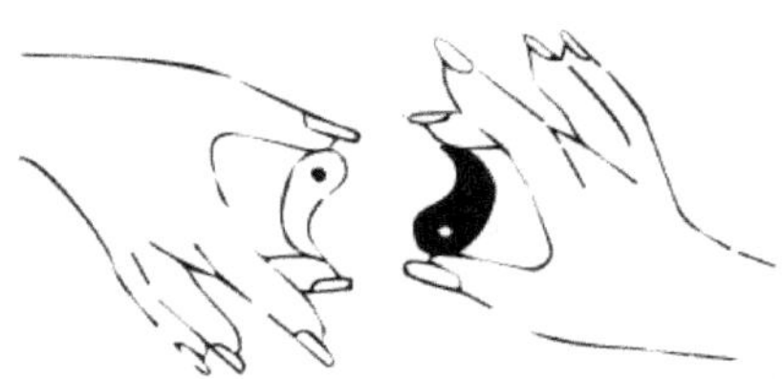

Unfinished Memory

he's thirty years of spilled ink...
across a million pages unfinished...
dreams left whole yet incomplete...
love that pain can not diminish...

an unfinished memory...

every quatrain filled with heat...
within every word unspoken...
a standard no one can meet...
left within my life as a token...

an unfinished memory...

haunting me in the present...
a face still traced in darkness...
like the moon at its crescent...
nothing matches the starkness...

but an unfinished memory...

Your Face

I think of you often in a world of broken dreams…
As I was catapulted down the road by so many
unseen things…
In shadows of the moon or the blinking of stars…
As I stumble in the darkness, there you are…
Though never far away in thought, you seem forever
out of reach…
Out of the past from which you came to the very soul
you breached…
In every panorama and nightmare come to pass…
I awake with silent panic that a glimpse might be the
last…
The last touch or chance to hear you, to see the smile
on your face…
Something to this day, in darkness, I can still trace…

The Compass

sometimes home is a place within a heart...
in a soul you cannot map or chart...
residing in a smile a laugh or a touch...
in residual tears wiped to much...
together or apart home will forever dwell...
in a presence no other is able to quell...
years come and go, changing ever more...
yet i still find that compass core...
direction and safety, balance with peace...
even in discord, sublime release...
when emotions bring to much feeling...
you're a space that remains unyielding...
allowing the unfiltered me a place to detach...
you settle the chaos without a scratch...
you are always the home i forever miss...
the place in entropy or ecstasy that is bliss...

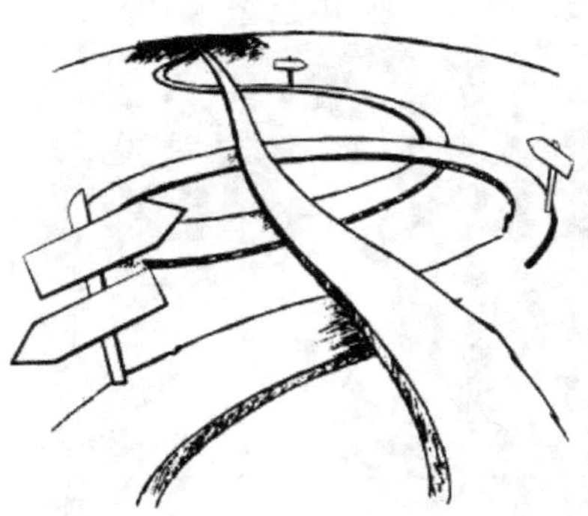

In the Chaos of Stasis

i see you in color when i close my eyes...
you echo within me, an imprint i can't deny...
a connection made long ago, still desired and loved...
in a silent and empty space it's been shoved...
no matter the heart put before me or the hand that
guided the way...
i looked for you within the shadows hoping you'd return
someday...
you always seem so far out of reach, yet tethered to my
soul...
i'd blink and see your face on a passing stranger in the
cold...
around every corner or isle walked, i saw you
everywhere..
in dreams of passion and the dark of sleepless nights
you were there...
in crowds of thousands, within an endless sea of faces...
i always thought i'd find you inside the chaos of stasis...
oh but yesterday, i saw your face on a screen i held in
hand...
and all the hollow empty spaces flooded with your voice
like sand...
filling every tiny crevice with a sound that feels like
home...
stitching up my soul in pieces, you said i'll not be
alone...

The Fire Entombed

it settled deep within her soul
a love that would burn for ages
constant and banked it smolders
inadequate words to fill the pages
flames that slumber in a coma
medicated into submission
a still and quiet love
dark flickers of heat for sublition
the grounding and foundation
for all who would come to pass
the inequity shining through
from the heart's darkest mass
one to regulate and diminish
when the fires rage beyond control
to match her in passion
let the fire breathe and unfold
measure up in greatness
stoke and entomb the fires
as all fall short in weakness
becoming kindling for the pyres

Beyond Measure

Beyond Measure

you've always been a light shining through my
darkest days... a presence within that loved me no
matter where i lay...

you've not been beside me in over a decade at best...
yet i still feel you when i close my eyes to the rest...

to say i never left you behind is a fragile state of
admission... you can't really leave if your heart and
soul are in submission...

you give me safety and control in a world far from at
peace... you stop me from spinning and bring me to
my knees..

you give me hope when life offers nothing but pain...
you give me sanctuary with nothing to gain...

a hollow of safety that takes only what i will give... a
tower that encompasses me and allows me to live...

you've held my heart from the day i first saw you...
you're the home that my soul always gravitates to...

its where i would choose to spend the rest of my
days... wrapped up in the color of your soul, within
your embrace...

i know how to live without you, i've done it
everyday... but missing you and loving you, that
never seems to go away...

there's nothing in my life that i haven't lost once or
even twice... loving you though, without presence, is
a loss beyond measure in its price...

www.ingramcontent.com/pod-product-compliance
Lightning Source LLC
La Vergne TN
LVHW021347200726
843509LV00014B/2714